DISCLAIMER

Please note that the publisher of this instructional book is NOT RESPONSIBLE in any manner whatsoever for any injury which may occur by reading and/or following the instructions herein.

It is essential that before following any of the activities, physical or otherwise, herein described, the reader or readers should first consult his or her physician for advice on whether or not the reader or readers should embark on the physical activity described herein. Since the physical activities described herein may be too sophisticated in nature, it is *essential that a physician be consulted.*

©**UNIQUE PUBLICATIONS INC., 1982**
All rights reserved
Printed in the United States of America
ISBN: 0-86568-006-X
Library of Congress No.: 76-55613

UNIQUE PUBLICATIONS

by DOUGLAS L. WONG

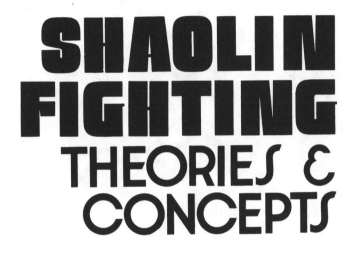

SHAOLIN FIGHTING
THEORIES & CONCEPTS

introduction

In this second book, "Shaolin Fighting Theories and Concepts," we will explore the many facets involved in Kung Fu. From the beginning stages of saluting to the advanced exercises used on the Kung Fu training equipment.

The chapter on Chinese Ranking will explain to the layman how respect is shown to each person through name rather than color ranking.

Chinese salutation will show some of the more popular gestures used in today's Kung Fu society.

The Hand Techniques will be discussed in detail. It will explain how the whole arm; from fingertip to the shoulder can be utilized into one main driving force. This will be used in conjunction with the various pressure points.

The main chapters will deal with two phases of fighting. The first will discuss the Basic Fighting Theories and Ground Fighting. Ground fighting is one of the techniques most useful and effective to use on the opponent. The Advance Fighting Principles will go into detail involving the use of Newton's Three Law on Motion theory. It will also describe a principle for attacker and defender alike.

The chapter on Internal System will describe the pathway of your breathing pattern.

And finishing off will be the Training Equipment. There are many types of equipment being used today. Some of the more useful ones are shown and demonstrated to fully outline a good training program.

May this book help provide much of the information needed for this ancient but fabulous art.

ABOUT THE AUTHOR

Sifu Douglas Lim Wong is an individual who enjoys his hobby to the fullest. His interest in this ancient art is one that encompasses the total aspect of Chinese pugilism.

Gung Fu is an art that is timeless, it deals with the events of life and its many consequences. It is a study of life from the day you are born to the day you die. The main branches of studies involved in this art are: Chinese Medicine, Physics, Philosophy, Logic, Psychology, Mathematics, History and also Self-Defense.

With so many subjects involved it is sure that a person must be well versed to ensure the proper teaching of each facet of this art. Also, you must study from a qualified instructor who is willing to share his wealth of knowledge.

He has had the privilege of studying under numerous fine instructors from various systems. He studied under Grandmaster Wong Ark Yuey of Los Angeles, California. Grandmaster Wong is one of the foremost practitioners in the Five Animals Style (Ng Ying Ga), and the Five Family Styles (Ng Ga Kin) as taught in China. At the advanced age of seventy-five years old, Grandmaster Wong is still actively teaching classes everyday. He later studied under Sifu Haumea "Tiny" Lefiti, a senior student of Grandmaster Ark Wong. Sifu Lefiti also studied in Taiwan learning the Mok Ga system and the White Crane system (Bai Hok Pai). He was head of the Polynesian-American Gung Fu Association until his death in 1973. From Si-Hing Walter Wong of Hong Kong, he studied the Wing Chun Chuan system learning the forms as well as the "Sticky Hand Training" known as "Chi Sao."

In 1973 under the tutelage of Master Share Lew, he was introduced to the higher levels of Gung Fu. From Master Lew he learned the Taoist internal system which includes Herbal Medicine, Meditation, and Taoist breathing exercises. Master Lew has been influential on Sifu Wong's knowledge. Master Lew teaches the Tao-on Pai (Tao Ga) system of Gung Fu and also the Choy-Li-Fut system as taught by his late uncle, Grandmaster Lew Ben (Lau Bun), the foremost authority on the Hung Sing Choy-Li-Fut system. Sifu Wong has also been exposed to the Yau Kung Mon style or the "Soft Hand Style," which is a relatively new art which has its origin from the infamous Bai Mei Pai or the forbidden "White Eyebrow Style." Yau Kung Mon was developed in Hong Kong by Grandmaster Ha Hoan. Sifu Wong has also been exposed to Northern Praying Mantis (Bak Tong Long Pai), Northern Sil Lum (Bak Sil Lum), Tai Chi Chuan (Grand Ultimate Fist), Bai Mei Pai (White Eyebrow System) Hsing-Yi Ching (Heart-Mind Boxing) and Bai Fu Pai (White Tiger System). Sifu Wong has also studied the Buddhist internal system and also the Iron Palm training.

From the total teaching of all his instructors he has formulated a new system of his own called the "White Lotus Flower Style" (Bai Ling Fa Pai). The White Lotus represents the purity of this new system among the many styles in existence today. During sunrise the Lotus flower opens up to the world to take in the events of the day. And when sunset approaches the flower closes and is at peace with the world through darkness. The White Lotus Flower is a Buddhist symbol of purity and happiness and has a very colorful history throughout the many eventful Chinese dynasties. Sifu Wong's interest in his heritage and culture was the key that opened the door of wisdom and knowledge to this fabulous art.

Being one of the most respected instructor's on the West Coast tournament circuit. He has produced Gung Fu's "Winningist Team" as quoted form one magazine article. He has achieved many milestones since opening his kwoon (studio) in January of 1973. Since then his Sil Lum Team led and captained by two senior students, Mr. Albert Leong and Mr. James Lew, have successfully captured every notable title in the Kata Division from Junior level to Black Belt level. At many tournaments they have swept every division entered. In Weapons competition they have been the most exciting group to watch. Never letting the people down for a minute, this group has completed and demonstrated throughout the United States and have appeared on many televison programs.

Sifu Wong has appeared in numerous movies and television programs, including the "Kung Fu" pilot film from Warner Bros. Studio; "That Man Bolt" from Universal Studio; "Apple Dumpling Gang" from Walt Disney Productions; and other members have appeared on television program such as "Ironside"; "Police Story"; "The Champion"; NBC Sport Show; "Philbin/Brown & Co."; "Sport Prep Show"; "Kung Fu" television series; "Secret of the Martial Arts" NBC series; "Medix" CBS Special; and many upcoming series.

Members have appeared in the Las Vegas Production of "Orient 75" at the Landmark Hotel and also at the Arizona State Fair. They have taken part in many community events and many benefits for underprivileged children foundations.

Sifu Wong has been chosen by Mayor Tom Bradley's Blue Ribbon Committee as the Kung Fu representative for the Martial Arts Advisory Board for the City of Los Angeles. He is also an overseas advisor for the Taiwan based Tang Shou Tao (Kung Fu) Committee of the Taipei Athletics Association.

The Sil Lum members have appeared in magazines such as Black Belt, Karate Illustrated, Official Karate, Oriental Art of Self-Defense, Inside Kung-Fu, Los Angeles Free Press, Karate-Ka, Single Register, Combat Magazine from England, Los Angeles Times, and many other local newspapers.

Within his Sil Lum Kung Fu school, have been trained such national champions as Albert Leong, James Lew, Robin Kane, Todd Takeuchi and Jimmy Brown, all of whom are known for their hand and weapon form expertise. In the fighting division he has Mr. William Henderson, the reigning U.S. Heavyweight Gung Fu Fighter in full contact matches. He is also one of the more popular fighters on the Karate tournament circuit.

Assisting Sifu Wong are three long time friends and fellow instructors Sifu Carl Totton, Sifu Tommy Ho and Sifu Wilson Quan. All four of the instructors have trained together at one time or another and have the combined experience of seven different styles of Gung Fu.

This is but a short biography on Sifu Wong, it can only give you a glimpse of his knowledge and his personality. As you read the following chapters in this book you will get a better insight into his personal teaching and a better understanding of this ancient Chinese art.

To my good friend and fellow martial artist — I wish him the best of luck and long life. May this book serve its purpose and help you understand the meaning of life and its many facets.

Eric Lee

To my Parents:

Thank you for guiding me down the road of life. Without your love and guidance the road to reality and happiness would have been an impossible dream.

THE SPIRIT OF REALITY

Young and beautiful
But yet knowing the way of life
The harshness and the bitterness
But yet knowing softness and gentleness
A description of a free soul
A soul in search of reality
But where are you bound?
How far is this road to reality?
Can it be found here?
Young and innocent
Yet old in the way of life
Help yourself by being yourself
For freedom is there
For happiness is there
For I am there!
For reality is there waiting for the two of us
Let us discover this wealth of life together
Together as one soul in the midst of reality
A reality which we can share in our heart and in our minds
Young and free
Yet searching for the way of life
Come with me to this land of peace
Come with me and discover that love is a reality
Come with me and uncover the meaning of reality
A reality that is in our soul

CONTENTS

History of Kung-Fu

Kung Fu, is one of the oldest fighting arts known to mankind. The date of its origins has been lost to antiquity. The term Gung Fu is a term coined by the Chinese who migrated to the United States in the 1800's during the California Gold Rush era and the building of the Transcontinental Railroad. There are many meanings for the term Gung Fu. The term Gung Fu means "hard work or task", or "always learning.

The more common terminology used in China is "Wu Shu" meaning Martial Art or "Chuan Fa" meaning Fist Fighting. Gung Fu has been pracitced and revised in China for over 4,000 years. It has evolved into an implement for health and self-defense. Gung Fu is one of the most complicated and effective systems of self-defense.

In the beginning of time man came into existence with inborn traits of survival. When confronted with a violent situation, a man learns to defend himself by using his body, or by picking up an object and converting it into a weapon.

The first punch or kick was considered the forerunner of many of today's fighting systems. From the days of the caveman to modern day society, men have regrouped and trained other human beings in a pre-arranged pattern of self-defense. Some styles were used by family members which was kept in their blood line while others taught it in their separate villages or area of living. No two styles were the same because both size and flexibility differed from person to person. Some were tall, short, light, heavy, slow, fast, and some were handicapped by physical injury. The techniques vary considerably through aging of time due to:

1) techniques improvement
2) mixing with other styles
3) misinterpretation of techniques
4) undertrained individuals that claim to be masters
5) deletion through mistrust

It all began, so the legends say, when a stern Indian monk noticed that his young Chinese disciples couldn't stay awake during the long and tiring meditation of the new religion, known as Chan or Zen Buddhism, he was trying to teach them. Not conditioned to endure the exhaustive meditative methods developed by the Hindu, Yogic and Buddhist monks of their Master's homeland, the young disciples seemed on the verge of failure in thier new undertaking. Realizing this, the first patriarch Bodhidharma took the initiative and introduced his frail disciples to an 18 movement exercise (18 Hand of Lo-Han) based on techniques discovered and developed beyond the Himalayas. Soon daily practice of the 18 movements strengthened the young disciples at the Sil Lum Temple enough to receive their Master's teachings thus sowing two seeds that the world would later know as Chan (Zen Buddhism) and Sil Lum Kung Fu.

Throughout history credit has been given to Bodhidharma (Dot Mor) as the creator of Sil Lum Kung Fu or the man responsible for introducing the Martial Art to China. This is not true. Gung Fu was already in existence long before Dot Mor arrived into China. His main contribution was the introduction of Chan (Zen) into the Sil Lum Temple.

Nearly 800 years after Dot Mor's death, monk Chueh Yuan, aided by two famous boxers of the time, Li, and Pai, set out to perfect a system which they felt was incomplete.

Upon completion of their work (done within the confines of the Sil Lum temple at Honan), Ch'ueh, Li and Pai unveiled a 170-movement system, subdivided into five animal styles — Crane, Dragon, Leopard, Snake and Tiger. Known as the Ng Ying Ga (Five Animal Style), they formed complementary styles, each with a different emphasis and approach.

The Crane, based on exercises to strengthen the sinews, stresses balance and quick foot movements; while the Dragon, from exercises for the spirit, stresses flexibility and graceful movement (the Dragon was an imaginary figure but it stresses the flowing spirit of the highly regarded legendary animal. On the other hand, the Leopard, a style that develops power and speed, it differs from the Tiger, a clawing style built on exercises for strengthening the bones. Finally, there was the Snake, based on exercises for chi or internal power, and concerned with pin-point hitting of vital spots.

Together, the five animals formed the complete basis of the art of Sil Lum Kung Fu. While countless other styles have sprung from modifications tailored to personal tsste or ability, the Five Animals System stands proudly as the complete and original Temple Style.

Chinese Ranking System

In the Chinese system there is no real ranking using belts as a distinction for denoting levels of achievement. The ranking system is based on the Chinese family structure which always places the elder as the head of the clan. The usage of title for each level was one of respect and obedience. The ranking is based on school age more than the actual age of the practitioner.

A younger student who enters a traditional Kung Fu school must always pay respect to his senior before himself. It does not matter whether the younger student is better than his senior, he still must pay respect to his elder. It is not a law but a rule followed by the philosophy and training given by each instructor. Your instructor will always be your instructor no matter how advanced you may become.

It is similar to a seed which must be watered and nurtured to grow to it's fullest potential. It was dedication on your instructor part that nurtured and cultivated your mind to absorb the information acquired through his years of training. Knowledge given to you to understand and to develop to the upmost for your own particular usages.

Knowledge is neutral, it has no will of its own to do anything. It is up to the individual to direct this knowledge into a productive channel. As the famous Zen Master Gasan has said;

A poor disciple utilizes a teacher's influence.

A fair disciple admires a teacher's kindness.

A good disciple grows strong under a teacher's discipline.

However a teacher is but a student of his students. He is guided by each and everyone of them.

The Chinese system uses the sash which is considerably wider than the Japanese belt (obi). The sash usually approximately 6" to 9" wide and from 9' to 14' long. The belt worn in China was used only for support of lower back due to exertion of motion on this area of the torso. It also controls the breathing center or the tan tien. The belt was also used to conceal small objects such as coins, darts, daggers and other weapons. Of course, the main purpose was to hold up the pants it-self. In China the pants worn in the olden days were loose pantloons that didn't restrict body movement.

The belt is called the loyality and filial piety belt which reminds one of his country and his ancestors.

Following is a flow chart containing the many titles of respect used in various Chinese systems. The giving of colored sashes is a modern day invention used by enterprising Americans as well as other groups spanning the world over. Remember ranking is not essential, it is each individual's knowledge that is important. A belt ranking is a material object and can be taken away from you, but the knowledge you have acquired is yours to keep and to use whenever the time may arrives.

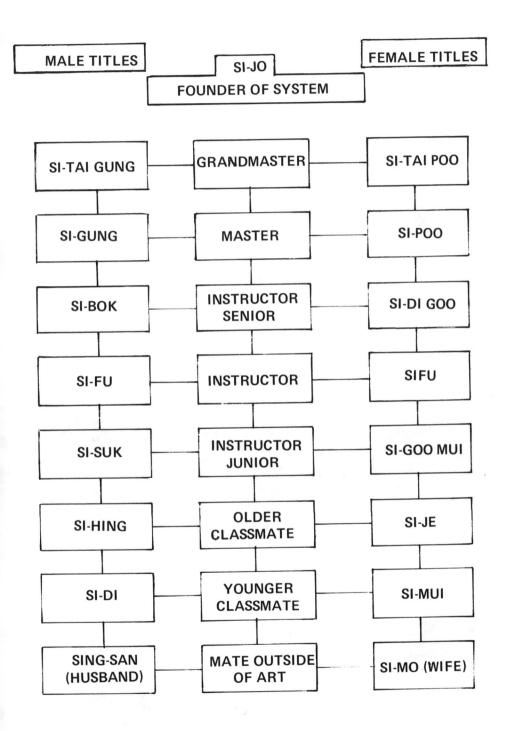

MALE TITLES	SI-JO FOUNDER OF SYSTEM	FEMALE TITLES
SI-TAI GUNG	GRANDMASTER	SI-TAI POO
SI-GUNG	MASTER	SI-POO
SI-BOK	INSTRUCTOR SENIOR	SI-DI GOO
SI-FU	INSTRUCTOR	SIFU
SI-SUK	INSTRUCTOR JUNIOR	SI-GOO MUI
SI-HING	OLDER CLASSMATE	SI-JE
SI-DI	YOUNGER CLASSMATE	SI-MUI
SING-SAN (HUSBAND)	MATE OUTSIDE OF ART	SI-MO (WIFE)

Chinese Salutation

Here are a variety of salutes from various styles. This is by no means all the salutes known, but these are the more well-known ones in use.

1

2

3

Salute — The Signs of Respect. The familiar left palm covering the right fist symbolizes the Shaolin boxing art and is imbued with the martial spirit. In the salute itself, the right hand represented the life line — power. The left hand symbolized the warmth and security of the sun. Combined, they showed respect for the individual.

Showing the people that you come unarmed and without hostilities. If forced to defend yourself, however, the right hand will be used for attacking while the left hand is used for blocking.

(1) Shaolin Salute
(2) Monk salute, hands together which represents a pacifist monk
(3) Another version of the Shaolin Salute

(4) From the White Eyebrow System or Bei Mei Pai, also used in the Soft Hand Style (Yau Kung Mon)
(5) Salute for the fighting monk
(6) Open salute used in Hung Gar style and other Gung Fu styles

4

5

6

Hand Techniques

In Kung-Fu the hand has a wide variety of applications, among them are: blocking, trapping, punching, deflecting, grabbing, pulling, clawing, ripping, pushing, poking, smashing, and raking. Some systems stress long hand techniques for greater strength and reach, while others rely on short hand tactics and rapid combinations. The ideal, of course, is to have both.

When speaking of the hand strikes we mean the entire length of man's natural weapon — the arm from shoulder to finger tips.

(1) The fingers are used for pinpoint striking and for interpreting an opponent's energy, because of their heightened sensitivity and feeling.

(2) The knuckles are used in a striking situation, there are many ways in using this type of strike. It can be used flush against the object or just a portion of the striking area in an upward strike or a downward motion to increase the power.

(3) The forearm is where the power is generated and are the primary blocking tools. They should be toughened through drills such as Dar Som Sing or "Striking the Three Stars." They can also be used to push a foe off balance.

(4) The wrist is the transmission through which energy and power are directed. Therefore, it must remain supple at all times so that the force proceeds unimpeded to the target.

(5) The elbow is very useful in short range situations. For instance a chest-level forearm block can easily be transformed into a follow-up elbow smash.

(6) The upper arm is that portion which provides the strength for extending or retracting a block or punch.

(7) The shoulder applies the power that has been gathered from the entire body, in the direction intended.

The different hand techniques and, obviously, their very descriptive names, were traced from various plants, animals and insects. For example, "Twin Dragons in Search of the Pearls", "Willow Palm," and "Monkey Steals the Peaches." A majority of the moves themselves were duplicated from birds and beasts, whereas, insects were admired for the immense strength they exhibited in proportion to their size, and plants for their essence or "inner" strength (i.e., the roots resembling a firm, solid "horse" or the flexible stalk, which represents the suppleness of the torso one should try to achieve).

There are three prerequisites for effective hand techniques: (1) speed, (2) strength, and (3) flexibility. Speed encompasses more than sheer velocity; it should also include an awareness of distance and timing. Strength is a function of one's build and musculature, yet it can be enhanced considerably by proper breathing and exercise. Flexibility is vital; without it, advantages in strength and speed are greatly diminished.

Ideally, the practitioner is relaxed until the exact moment of impact of a block or strike; at that instant all his energy should be focussed upon a single point. Failure to remain calm and collected has a number of detrimental effects. One is fatigue. If the practitioner is tense all the time, energy will be dissipated to no avail. Also, if a strike is initiated with the muscles tight, it will be too slow to be effective. The muscles and wrists must be loose in order to generate adequate power for an effective blow. Lastly, if one approaches a combat situation relaxed and free from anxiety, it has a psychological effect on his opponent.

The real key, however, is concentration. The mind must be free from all outside distractions, so that the different parts of the body can be coordinated into an efficient fighting machine. Advanced techniques, such as simultaneous blocking and punching, require a tremendous amount of body control, balance, and a sharpening of all the senses.

The hand is capable of blocking 80% of all attacks including punches, kicks and weapon attacks. The rest depends on maneuverability and the mind to out think your opponent.

Hand Theory

For every strike designate a target
For every target a reason
For every reason a purpose!

Do not waste motion — keeping the hand flexible and in condition are the upmost in hand training.

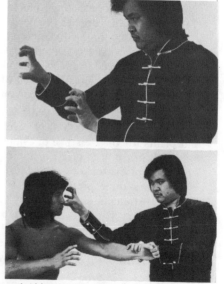

(Above) Tiger Claw. The fingers are spread and bent at the knuckles to emulate a claw; they need to be strengthened by proper exercise, also, this technique employs ripping, tearing and raking motions and can be quickly converted into a grab and palm strike.

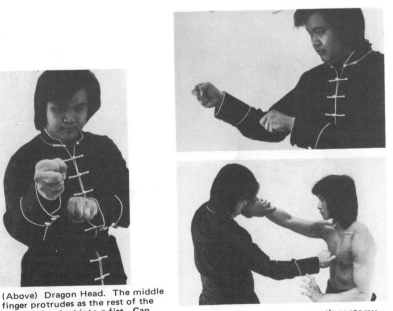

(Above) Leopard Punch. Power is concentrated in a brief area by clenching the fingers at the fore-knuckles and keeping the wrist straight so that it can flow unhindered from the entire body. This strike is modeled after a leopard's paw and is used in close-range situations for attacking small openings.

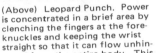

(Above) Dragon Head. The middle finger protrudes as the rest of the hand is clenched into a fist. Can be used for pinpoint striking to various pressure points on the opponent's anatomy — usually the solar plexis or heart area.

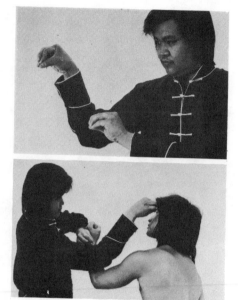

(Above) Crane's Beak. The fingertips are gathered together to form the striking surface which represents a crane's beak. The strike is delivered with pecking and poking motions: and the primary areas of attack are the eyes, temple or other highly vulnerable spots.

(Above) Snake Strike. Using the index and middle finger together as a striking surface, this represents the striking tongue of a snake. This is used primarily for pressure points striking.

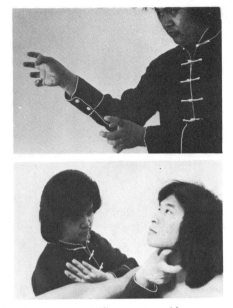

(Above) Eagle Claw. Here the index finger and middle fingers are used in conjunction with the all-mighty thumb. The three projections are used to attack soft and unprotected portions of the body, most likely the throat. It can wipe out the windpipe or juggler veins, while the other hand keeps your opponent at bay.

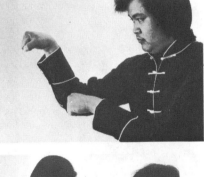

(Above) Elephant Trunk. The hand is clenched in a fist and turn toward the opponent. The hand represents the trunk of an elephant. One hand is used for hooking and the other hand for punching. The fist is used for hooking and punching while the forearm is used for blocking.

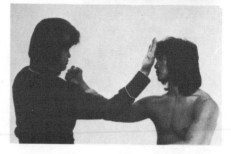

(Above) Back Hand. Attack with
the back of the hand, using the
knuckles as the striking area. This
method is widely used for attacks
to the head or for circling around
techniques thrown by your opponent.

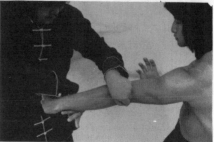

(Above) Mantis Claw. The index
and middle finger are held in imi-
tation of the insect's feelers. This
technique is applied with a hooking
— not grabbing — motion, against elbows or other joints. With the free hand applying pressure in the opposite direction, it is quite simple to render a limb useless almost
instantly.

(Above) Ax Hand. The fingers are held together and used for striking in angular strikes similar to the "Willow Palm."

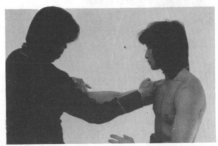

(Above) Sun Fist. A power strike that can be effectively used almost anytime. It is called the Sun Fist because it represents the radiant power of the sun; which in this case is the intrinsic energy, chi, that has been applied with either an upward or downward motion, depending upon which direction you want the energy to flow.

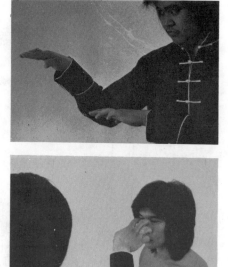

(Above) Twin Dragons in Search of the Pearls. The two fingers represent a pair of dragons in flight, and the "pearls" are the eyes. Only the index and middle finger are used and they are angled slightly to reinforce the power of the strike. If the fingers were held straight, they might slip off the area of attack; whereas in this manner, they fit the natural curvature of the face.

(Above) White Snake Head. One must be especially aware of proper angling when using this four finger strike, so that it doesn't just glance off a heavily protected area of the face such as the forehead. Be sure that the opposite hand is ready to block an attempted counter.

(Above) Willow Palm. The four fingers are held in close combination and the thumb is curved under the edge of the "Willow Leaf." The main striking area is the base of the palm and the side of the hand, which pulls the opponent off balance in the direction of the strike — thus doubling the force of the blow.

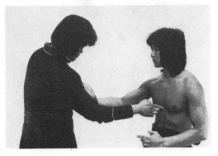

(Above) Finger Strike. The first finger is used for striking implement, the whole hand is tense and is braced against the striking finger. This is used for striking pressure points and soft area of the body.

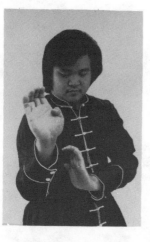

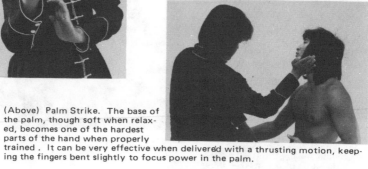

(Above) Palm Strike. The base of
the palm, though soft when relaxed, becomes one of the hardest
parts of the hand when properly
trained . It can be very effective when delivered with a thrusting motion, keeping the fingers bent slightly to focus power in the palm.

(Above) Elbow strike. The
whole arm and the elbow
joint is used for striking. The
strike can be used sideways
and upwards but for in-
fighting only.

(Above) Wrist strike. The back of the wrist is used in this instance; it is very delicate, so proper conditioning is a prerequisite for attempting such a strike. The wrist strike can be applied to the temple for high attacks, or for a low attack to the groin.

(Above) Ridge hand. The inside edge of the hand is used for striking. The ridge hand is used for long range striking.

(Above) Reverse Ridge Hand.
The back of the hand is used
for striking. This strike is
similar to the ridge hand but
the difference is the range
it can reach compared to the former. The reverse ridge can be used to hook
the back of the head — use opposite hand for blocking.

(Above) Phoenix Eye.
The index finger protrudes
to form an accurate and
powerful striking surface. This technique is used for attacking the throat or
Adam's Apple; and it is said to be taken from the Phoenix, a mythical bird
who was consumed by fire and reborn out of its own ashes.

(Above) Back Fist. The back of the hand is used as the fist is clenched. The angle of attack is used from a high position to a lower position. As shown on the right it is used for striking the shoulder area to dislocate the joints.

(Above) Monkey Paw. The fingers are dropped down and are facing your opponent. The usage of hooks and blocking are the main application.

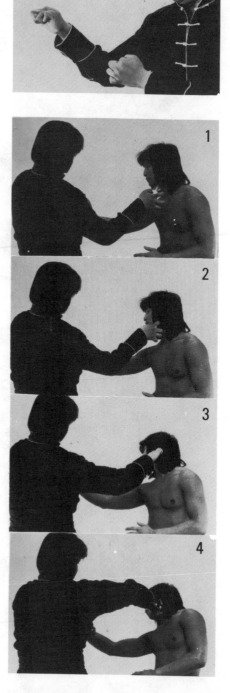

Ginger Fist. The strike is used as a hook and then as a strike in the same motion. (1) Start with an open hand grab. (2) Lock under the jaw bone. (3) Twist the hand and use the first two fingers as a strike. (4) Continuing the motion finish off by rolling the rest of the fingers into his face. This acts as four strikes at once and can render a person helpless if done properly.

White Ape Offers a Cup of Wine. The hands are formed as if holding a cup in your hand using the inside palm and upper finger region for strikes. (1) Ready position — opponent throws left punch. (2) Before punch reaches its point (destination) the right hand is dropped on top while the left arm approaches the throat. (3) The right hand grips and pushes downward while the left hand grabs the throat. (4) The final step is to extend both arms — thus causing a double impact strike to the neck region.

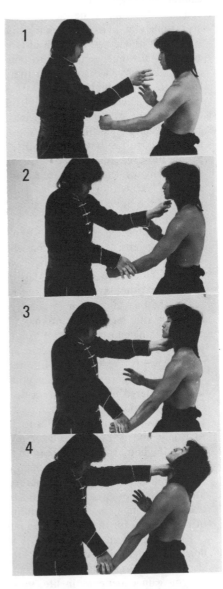

Philosophy and Mental Training

The mind is a complicated subject. Even today, scientists cannot fully explain how it functions or why. The Chinese have always considered the mind the most important part of the body. It controls everything you do or are planning to accomplish in the future.

In the Chinese art, we have different breathing exercises to make us aware of our inner sense and to improve our outlook on life. In Chinese philosophy, we are taught there are two parts of the brain. The first part of the brain, or the left side, controls our mechanical processes such as walking, working, lifting and many other everyday activities. But the other side, which is the Psychic Center, is the part that gives certain people their ESP ability, the ability to move objects with their mind, to heal, and many other such phenomena. To the Chinese people however, this is very normal. The Masters of Kung Fu can perform many of these feats, but they are very reluctant to teach this phase of the art. This part has caused much trouble in the past, and many of the older, traditional Sifu are not willing to teach this phase, of even demonstrate that it does exist.

I have witnessed many of these so called phenomena and can explain why it happens. It is something which any person can learn if his instructor is willing to teach him. I was very lucky because I was helped by or offered help by three Masters of the internal systems. I was amazed or I should say shocked at what I saw and what I learned. The fallacy of one taking ten to twenty years to learn the internal is to cover the true facts. The internal, if your teacher is willing to teach, can be learned in two years if you are a fast learner, and five years if you are a slow learner. But again, it depends on how intense your instructor wants to get involved into this phase of the art.

The main requirement is that you are mentally ready to accept what is being offered to you. Many a time we had nothing but our faith in our teacher to carry us through, but it was well worth it. Much of the teaching was oral in order for us to pay closer attention, and also for us to truely understand the subject. Much of the information you have seen in the book is being exposed to the public for the first time.

This phase of the art is still being kept alive in the Orient, but very few people are teaching these methods in the open here in the United States. Even fewer can even claim to know this system. Many that do teach this system are looked down upon because they consider this part of the art only for their immediate family member or their top disciple.

Knowledge is an object which is readily available for anyone to understand and to utilize for any certain goal or enlightenment. But it is also a dangerous substance which can change a persons way of thinking. As you gain experience in life, you will soon view life as a stepping stone to yet a higher level of learning.

No one person can claim to know the wisdom of the universe, the vastness, the emptiness, the happiness, the sadness, the sorrow or the joy of life, for all of this is beyond human description. We have no true words to describe this concept to its fullest. But each of us, in our own hearts and minds, can enjoy these moments and relish these thoughts for the rest of our lives.

Life is a precious possession. A person should be able to live in harmony with all life around him. There are times when it is necessary to protect yourself and your family. At those times you must decide to restrain your opponent, to cripple him or take his life. This is a very hard decision, and each person must learn to choose for himself. Is there a choice or not? Can the trouble be worked out, or do you really have to protect yourself to the utmost.

Basic Fighting Principles and Ground Fighting

In many self defense courses, ground techniques are the least emphasized. This is due to the complexity involved with the body. In order to be properly trained for techniques, a person must be agile enough to roll, tumble, and must be capable of taking a fall. The main requirement is to have your body conditioned to the point where it can maneuver itself to any given position, whether it be an in the air kicking, standing on solid ground, or maneuvering on the ground.

A take down is an after product of your initial attack. Usually a technique can't be applied until your attacker is slowed down or stunned for a split second. The follow-up is important because a person is really not stopped by just one blow. A follow-up technique is required in order to attain full control of your opponent.

There are many ways of setting your opponent up for a take-down technique. Understanding your opponents body motion and weak points are very important.

(1)   Is the opponent's center of gravity high, low, or changing?
(2)   What type of attack is thrown at you — kicks, punches, sweeps, etc.?
(3)   Is the opponent fast or slow? Strong or weak?
(4)   Is he an experienced fighter? (Watch his movement closely.)
(5)   Is he a stationary fighter? Or is he constantly moving?

Many of these questions are applied when sizing up your opponent. Some will seem ridiculous to you, but you will be surprised at how many people don't understand these questions.

Now to recap each question?

(1)   Center of gravity is very important!
   (a)   A person's center of gravity affects his balance and mobility. When a person stands upright — his center of gravity is higher.
   (b)   If he fights from a stance position his body is more stable and his center of gravity is lower.
   (c)   If he is bouncing around like a boxer, his center of gravity is constantly shifting.
(2)   Types of attacks!
   (a)   Punching — is he punching high, low, hooking or a rapid combination or is he doing traditional one step fighting? It is important to remember that you can offset his attack if you understand the type of offense that he is throwing your way.
   (b)   Kicks, sweeps (leg attacks).
      When an opponent attacks with his leg he is usually positioned on one leg while kicking with the other leg, or the double leg attack while in the air or even on the ground. Your reflexes must be to the point where you can detect the oncoming attacker and prepare to counter by slightly retreating and then countering by jamming or blocking his legs.

(3)　Your opponent's strength and speed!

    (a)　Remember each person in the world is different. The weakness of an opponent is usually given away in his first initial attack. You can tell if he is strong or weak with that first blow. A strong opponent is one that you have to defend by using more angles, while a weaker opponent can be taken by either straight line or angular attack.

    (b)　Speed is an important factor in countering. Remember that a straight line is the shortest distance between two points, but this can only be effective if a person knows how to use circular angles to offset his opponent's attack. You can use speed on a slower opponent but not to the point where you become careless and bypass his attack and leave yourself wide open for a counter. If a person is faster than you, you may have to play possum to draw your opponent into you before you can counter attack. At certain times you may have to sacrifice yourself to the point where you will receive a few blows to accomplish what you set out to do. As my teacher, Mr. Haumea Lefiti, used to repeat over and over again, "It is not how much you can dish out, but how much you can take before you overcome your opponent. Remember that no man is invincible, you will have to accept the fact that you will get hit, slapped, kicked, spit-up on, and stomped into the ground. Once you attain this realization you will be at peace within yourself."

(4-5)　You can watch an opponent and know if he is a well-trained fighter or not, if he is faking, you will be able to tell when you make the initial moves. A good fighter knows that a moving target is harder to hit, so he will be constantly moving and using angles on his opponent.

These are but a few brief descriptions on understanding your opponent. The following techniques are based on take-downs and ground fighting. The advantages of the techniques are that they are seldom seen or used because of the body condition involved in using the technique. Also because people don't believe in fighting on the ground. However, on the street anything can happen.

The disadvantage is if you are slow and not fully trained to accomplish these techniques. Try to find a school that teaches you how to fight standing, on the ground, and other situations. Make sure that they teach you the fundamentals of falling and rolling, without that you will definitely injure yourself unnecessarily. Most competent schools will teach you these techniques and not just say, "Well we don't teach it here, besides you don't need it, we always win our fights standing up." Don't be taken in by these inexperienced people!

1

Ready position.

2

Opponent throws a punch which is blocked with an outside wrist block.

Defender pulls leg up to set up for a sweep.

3

The instep hits the opponent behind the knee area which causes the opponent to be off-balance for a split second.

4

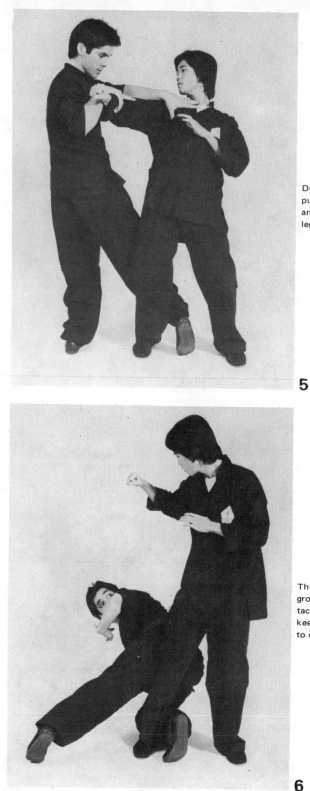

Drop his leg down, the defender pulls his opponent backwards and braces his leg behind the leg of the opponent.

5

The defender then drops to the ground and maintains eye contact with the opponent but also keeping the bottom leg hooked to opponent.

6

Swing his leg upward and down
of the knee area while the other
leg pushes outward on the bottom.

7

Completing the take-down by
spinning into the opponent.

8

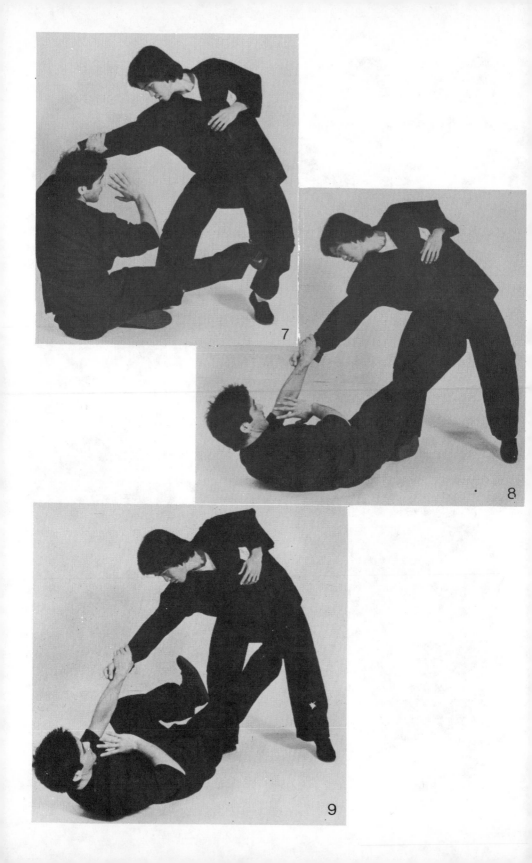

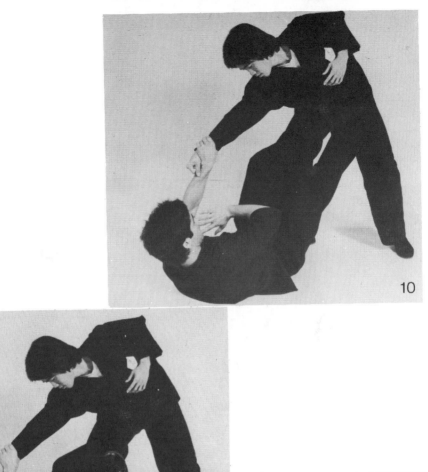

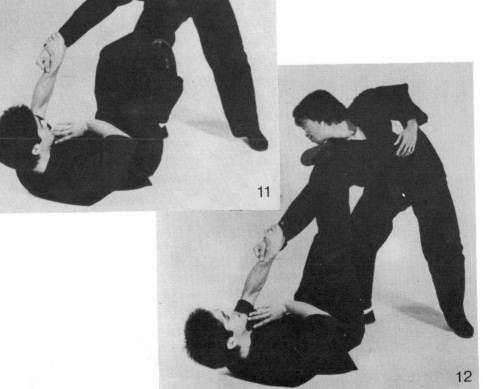

5

6a

6b.

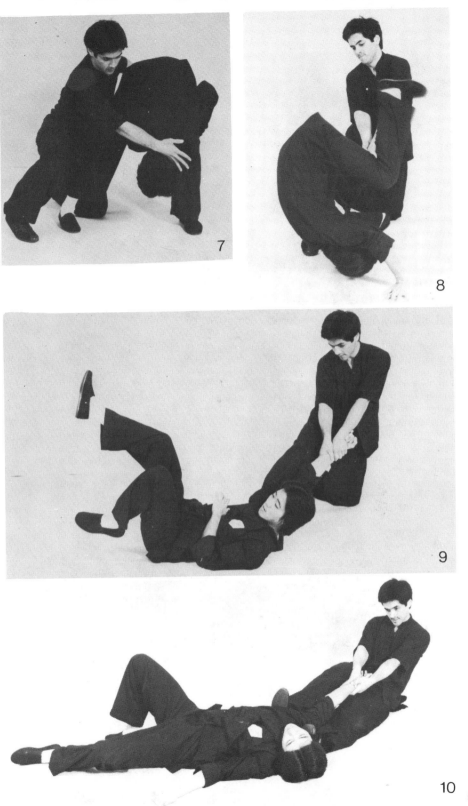

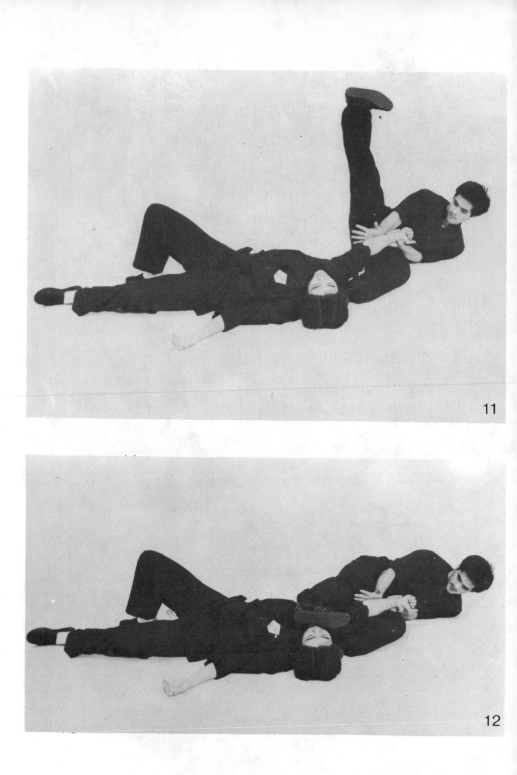

11

12

Internal System

The internal system is the most highly kept secret in the Chinese culture. It has been referred as the secret of eternal youth, the controller of the mind, the unstopable force, and many other such terms. The people who knew the internal were usually regarded as supermen because they could perform tasks that no other human being was capable of performing. The many feats witnessed by the population bewildered them, and they considered that the men were helped by the Gods.

The internal system is available to anyone who is willing to go through the training, provided there is a qualified instructor willing to teach you. There are many people claiming to teach the internal energy or Nui Gung, but very few can produce it or even explain the reasoning behind it. The energy is one that every person is capable of producing but with the proper sequences only. There are many different breathing exercises that cultivate the chi as well as other exercises that develop it to the point where you can use it for healing.

Healing is the main purpose of the internal system besides providing good health to the practitioner. Healing is part of the art that each teacher must strive for. The healing can be done by using acupuncture that is the use of a needle inserted into various points throughout the body and to regulate the flow of energy or chi. There are many points throughout the body that is necessary to learn before processing to the treatment. Healing with the needle is not always possible so we use what is known as the Healing Hand or using the hand or fingers as the implement in relieving of certain ailment and pain. The hand acts as the feeler for any over abundant of energy or under abundant which ever the case may be.

The beginning of the internal exercises is to start with the proper breathing methods. The Taoist internal breathing is done in the lower abdominal region or the area below the navel about 3" called the tan tien. The pathway is as follows: inhale through the nose but bypass the chest region. Push the air down into the tailbone area and then up the spinal cord to the top of the head. The chi then goes to the front part of the forehead known as the third eye. This area is the concentration point known as the psychic center.

After learning the internal, one is capable of healing some of the more common ailments affecting people. You can also start to sense many of the objects around you, and you will build up the senses of your body so you can feel another person's body heat coming toward you from any direction. You can also see different colors of the aura surrounding a person in that way, you can tell if he is angry, scared, kind, or whatever.

The internal is also an art that is deadly because of the medical application learned for healing can be used in killing. The system is involved with the Delayed Death Touch or Dim Mak. Many demonstrations have been done to show the internal system and while most people are amazed at the feats accomplished, the internal is still difficult to believe or understand.

Remember, it takes two people to have a fight. If one of them walks away, where is the fight? The fight that you prevent physically can be more of a battle in your own mind. But remember, life is a precious commodity, not something you can buy and sell. If you have a good instructor, he will teach you both mental and physical control of your body. A good instructor can show you ways of restraining your opponent or slowing him down without causing permanent damage. Also, he will teach you how to handle yourself when the odds are against you and when you have no choice but to take a persons life. It is up to the teaching he has given you, what is in your own heart, and the destiny you choose for yourself.

Advanced Fighting Principles

Fighting principles are the hardest ideas to explain but the actual fighting principles are simple but very effective.   The main concern in fighting is to use the minimum movement and strength, but to get the maximum effective effect without wearing yourself out. No one system can claim to have all the fighting techniques or principles together but in the following chapter you will be exposed to some of the more sophisticated movements used in the White Lotus System.

Gung Fu movements can be broken down into two components or motions, linear motion or straight line, and circular motion or circling angle. Every motion used in fighting, such as forward, backward, sidestep, pushing, pulling, and sweeping is involved with linear and circular motion. Sometimes a combination of both is necessary to overcome your opponent and to give yourself the upper hand in any fighting situation.

Natural moves are the most effective fighting implement. No one needs to be trained in something that is already second nature to him. Many students however, make things so complicated that they defeat their own purpose. A simple gesture of the hand, a twist of the wrist, a snapping of a finger, a sliding of the arm, all these are very natural and useful for any self-defense movement. The practioners must learn to relax when they are fighting, while keeping calm and composed

On guard position.

Opponent throws right punch toward opponent's head which is met by a left sliding punch making sure the body is leaning away from the punch.

Breathing is also an important part of fighting. Without the proper technique of breathing, you might be winded before the fight is over, and if your opponent is in better condition, he will overcome you very rapidly. Low abdominal breathing can keep you one step ahead of your opponent and protect the vital organs located in your lower torso area. The mouth must also be closed with the tongue curled and touching the roof of your mouth. This circulates the saliva in the mouth and keeps it moist through any activity you are participating in.

When fighting an opponent, set up safety zones around your body and know where each zone is and when it is necessary to respond to certain attacks. When a person attacks your body, there is no need for you to chase the punch. It will come to you eventually. Remain calm and keep your eyes on your opponents waist since this is the main gap between the upper and lower torso. The body must move before the kick or punch can be delivered, therefore, if you notice which half is attacking, then you can be ready to defend against it.

Following are a few principles used in fighting with certain rules pertaining to Newton's Three Law on motion.

(1) A body at rest tends to remain at rest and a body in motion tends to remain in motion in a straight line and at constant speed when left alone (that is, when it is not acted upon by some unbalanced force).

(2) When an unbalanced force acts upon a body it will change the velocity of the body in the direction of the force. (The change of velocity will be in direct proportion to the size of the force and to the time during which it acts on the body, and in inverse pro-

The right hand then converts into a reverse grab and the hand continues to slide upward toward opponent's punch.

portion to the mass of the body.

(3)   For every action there is an equal and opposite reaction. Also involved are "Potential energy and Kinetic energy."

A body can be divided into many segments — when a force hit a body at certain area the force can dissipate the opponent's force in half or totality. To reach the opponent's body, a line must be drawn from your striking implement to the area intended to be struck. For example from point A to point B the shortest pathway would be a straight line.

NEWTON LAW

CG = center of gravity
CP = center point (central point)

No motion still

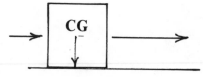

In motion, body will travel in a straight line

Outside force (40 lb.)

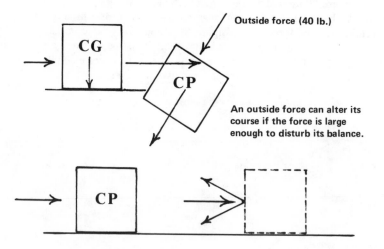

An outside force can alter its
course if the force is large
enough to disturb its balance.

10 lb. force
strike object

Bounce off the force

The shortest distance between A & B is a straight line.

If a wall was put inbetween points A & B — then the force A would be bounced off to the side if C is strong enough to withstand the force of the blow. Upon impact the force is sent into a new direction.

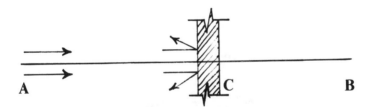

Now the shortest path from A to B is a circle which goes around point C or the wall.

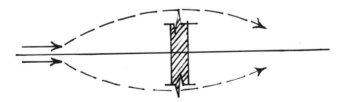

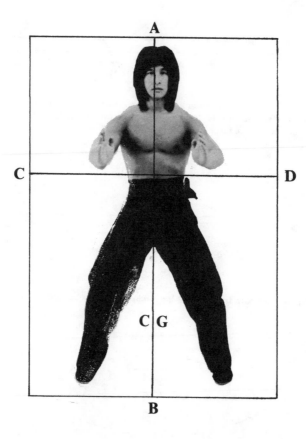

The body is divided into 4 main components having the center of gravity as the main essence of balance for the entire body. Knowing the point which controls a person's center of gravity can be very useful in fighting.

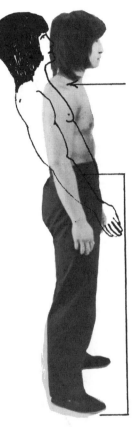

When a person sees an object come toward his head, like a punch, he tends to lean back away from the punch. This then leaves his lower limb vulnerable for an attack.

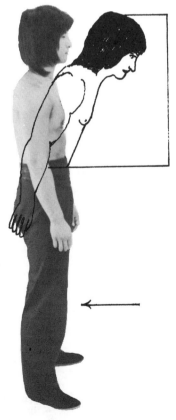

Then if a kick is thrown at the lower limb the person tends to pull back but the top half will lean slightly forward. Attack to the upper torso is very effective at this time.

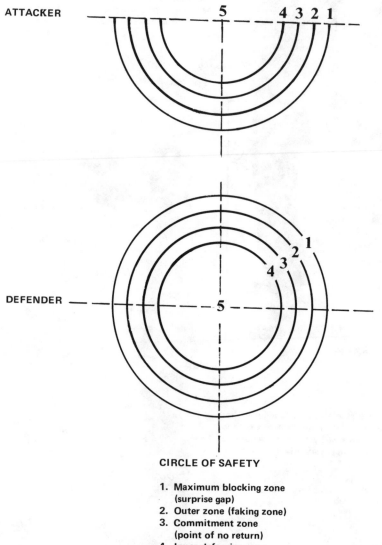

SEMICIRCLE OF ATTACK

1. Maximum striking zone
2. Committed zone
3. Direction zone
4. Minimum punching zone
   (initial zone)
5. Center — source of energy

ATTACKER

DEFENDER

CIRCLE OF SAFETY

1. Maximum blocking zone
   (surprise gap)
2. Outer zone (faking zone)
3. Commitment zone
   (point of no return)
4. Inner defensive zone
   (clinging)
5. Center — body minimum
   blocking zone

1 2 3 4 5

1. MAXIMUM POINT — OUTER ZONE: outside line impact point
2. OUTER CIRCLE: final impact point
3. MIDDLE ZONE: initial impact area
4. INNER ZONE
5. SOURCE OF FORCE

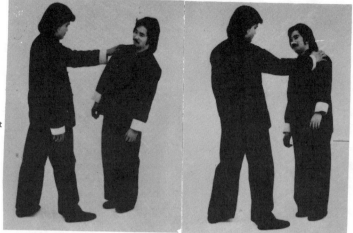

BALANCE TEST (Right) — Understanding the pressure in usage against an opponent's balance and center of gravity. (1) Pushing the side, the balance is off-balance. (2) Opposite side the same.

Top Gate

Middle Gate

Lower Gate

left side | right side

Natural standing position

Using fingertip push the front,
and the back is off-balance.

Pull in, and the balance is
offcenter

(Above) — Ready position.

(Above) — Opponent throws a right punch to Sifu Wong's stomach region which is met with a sucking action which dissipates the power of the punch.

(Above) — Ready position.

(Above) — Opponent throws a high punch which is deflected with an inside palm block.

(Below) — Before the whole hand can concentrate it's power on the body, Sifu Wong twists his body toward opponent which deflects the punch away from the body.

3

(Below) — Sifu Wong then uses a Tiger Claw to the groin region.

4

(Below) — The left hand is then circled up and onto the elbow joint with a Mantis Hook Hand.

3

(Below) — Now deliver a Phoenix Eye punch to the eyes or temple region.

4

1

LOW FAKE into HIGH ATTACK. Ready position (above).

2

(Above) — The attacker throws his right fist into the opponent's face while also drawing the back leg in toward the front. The fist makes the opponent pull his face back.

(Above) — While the opponent is backing up, release a sliding heel kick to the knee region.

(Above) — Drop the leg down, prepare the hand for any type of attack.

(Above) — Block opponent's front hand with a palm block and prepare a back hand fist to the opponent's head.

(Above) — Complete the final stage by striking into the temple.

Fighting position.

Opponent throws punch which is met with a double outside palm block.

The right hand controls the punching hand while the left hand slides into the eyeball.

The spear hand is then dropped on top of the punching arm and the left hand converts into a fist.

4

Final stage when the punch connects to the temple area.

5

Double Tiger Strike

Ready position.

Ready position.

Block the punching hand with an inside palm block.

Opponent's punch is met with a double outside palm block.

After deflecting the punch, Sifu Wong uses a double tiger strike to the face and groin area simultaneously.

Right hand comes to upper part of the punching arm — other hand on the elbow joint using the two hands in a scissor lock effect which jolts the arm as if done hard enough to snap the arm.

Yank the hand and convert the hand into a fist and punch the head region.

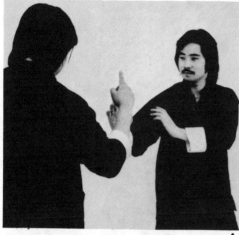

Ready position.

1

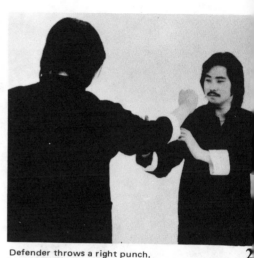

Defender throws a right punch.

2

Continue the hooking hand inward and
upward.

5

Hook pass the body and. . . .

80

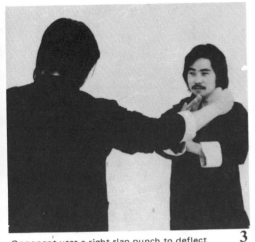

Opponent uses a right slap punch to deflect
the hand sideward. **3**

Going the direction of block, the hand
swings back while the other hand deflects
the punch. **4**

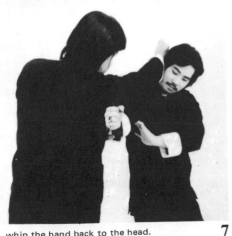

. . . whip the hand back to the head. **7**

(Right 3 pictures) — Fighting position.

Right punch is evaded by a lean back but is deflected to the side.

Now sliding the leg to the side, pull your opponent's toward you; which throws opponent off balance.

HAND STRIKING. (Below) — This series show how a single strike can be converted into six strikes or more on the same offensive move.
Fingertip Strike is used to feel the distance of opponent's body.

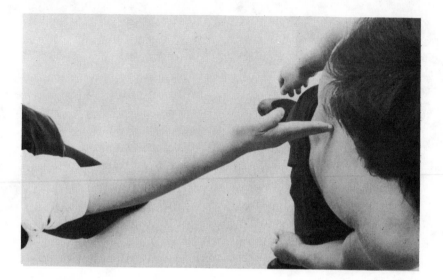

Converting into a **Leopard Paw** strike with the foreknuckles.

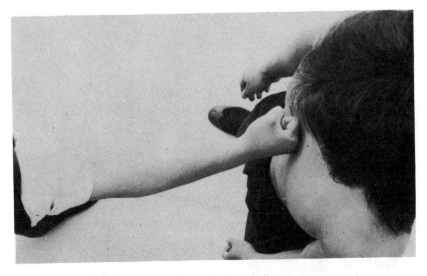

After striking, change into a **Sun Fist Strike** using the internal energy.

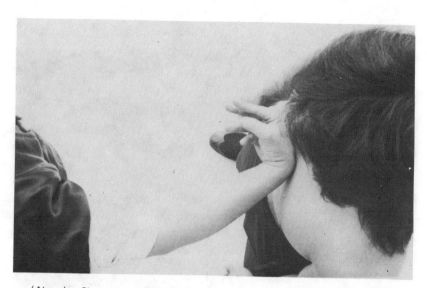

(Above) — Change into a **Wrist Strike** which is done with a snapping motion which shakes up the balance of the body.

(Above) — Forearm strike which uses the front portion of the forearm and is very powerful.

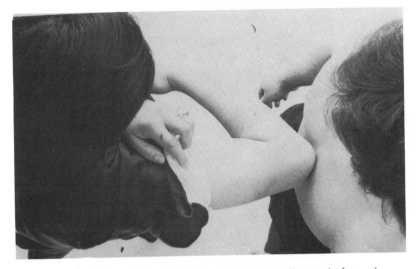

(Above) — Change into **Elbow Strike** using the tip of the elbow and a forward thrusting motion.

Knowing how to maneuver the body is one of the greatest asset in fighting. A simple punch to the body can be reguided into a less offensive movement.

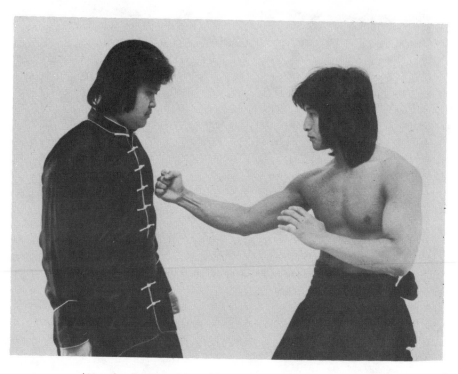

(Above) — Ready position with opponent throwing a right punch.

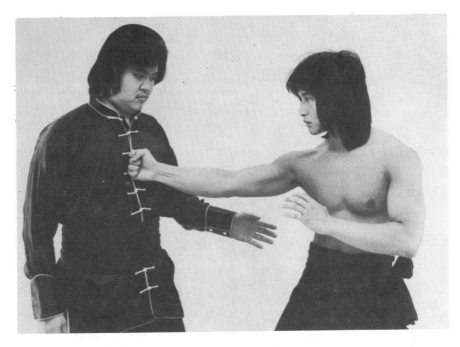

(Above) — As the punch approaches it's target the defender simply turns his body sideway and brushes the punch to the side. (Below) — The final stage is to let the punch pass by and be prepared to throw your own offense.

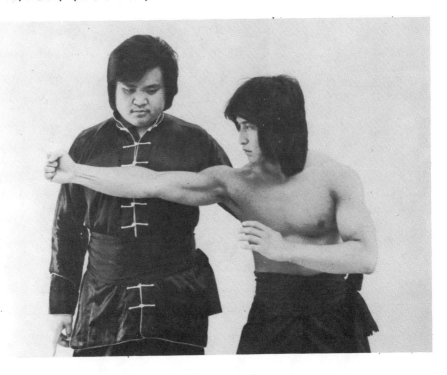

Side view of a punch by using deflection and grab.

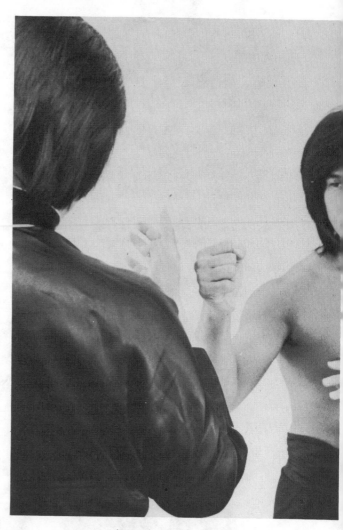

(Above) — Ready position.

(Left) — Opponent throws a punch which is met with a wrist block.

(Right) — To deflect the force of the punch drop your hand downward which redirects the opponent's power downward.

(Left) — Still continuing the motion turn the hand over which converts the block into a grab.

(Right) — Now using the left hand as a checking hand, the grab is converted into an inside ridge strike to the throat.

Training Equipment

Training equipments come in many various shapes and forms. In the martial art field there are many such implements that are very large and bulky while others are small and portable. The Chinese training equipment are very elaborate and covers many aspect in conditioning the human torso.

The most popular and handiest equipment are the various sizes of sandbags. They are used for slapping, poking, grabbing, punching, drilling and chopping. Some are laid on top of an object and are pounded upon while others are thrown in the air and grabbed when airborne.

Other schools use the different container which holds various substance to condition the hand such as sand, small pebbles, dried beans, and then various mixture of the mentioned items. There are different stages for this type of training and preparation is a must for the beginners. This type of training conditions the hand from the fingertips up to the elbow.

The training dummies are used to build-up the power of one's punches and kicks. It is used for hand coordination, distancing, spacing, sensitivity, conditioning and focussing.

The dummies were used in various ways in China. Probably the most famous were the ones used at the Sil Lum Temple (Shaolin Temple). Near the completion of their graduating test, the young monks were to enter the Hall of the 108 Wooden Men. In the passageway were 108 dummies set up in such a way that it attacked from every conceivable angle and wielding different weapons in it's midst. Once the young monk candidate got through this hall, he then had to remove the urn blocking the passageway to the outside world.

The dummies in the hallway were triggered off by the weight of a person entering the hall and others controlled by monks behind the dummies. They used weapons such as swords, staffs, clubs, and other implements of destruction.

The most familiar dummy today is the Wing Chun Mook Jong, or the Wooden Man Dummy. There are 108 movements used by the practitioner to fully utilize this equipment. This developed the sense of fighting by using angular attacks and applying power into each strike. The lower portion of the dummy is used to provide the proper distancing and entrapment of the opponent's leg before applying a kick to the area.

The dummies were used to create the feeling of fighting a live opponent because the dummy was capable of taking more physical abuse than the human body. Therefore, it was more practical to work with, especially if you lacked a training partner. Solo exercises and endless combinations are used on this equipment; of course, actual fighting is still the best way of improving oneself. Feeling the power of one's blows and how much he can actually take is a very important factor involved in using this equipment.

The above mentioned equipment was mainly used for the upper torso or arm regions. For the legs there is various equipment, but the most useful and the most difficult one to master is the Mui Fa Joh or the Plum Flower Piles (or Stumps). Here they learn the different pattern of horse shifting from one area to the next since each stump was of different heights and size. This development of the horses is more readily adaptable for any situation whether it is on level ground or uneven terrain.

Today many of these equipments are not being utilized due to the lack of knowledge or instruction and also unable to produce such equipment. After working with the equipment the herbal medicine, Dit Da Jow, or Medicated Striking Wine, is applied to the striking surface. The Dit Da Jow comes in many different formulas; some used in conjunction with the dummy training while others are used for the Iron Palm or hand training.

The Iron Palm medicine is the strongest one to use in this phase of the art. The medicine penetrates the skin, tissue, muscle, veins, arteries down to the bone itself. It toughens and conditions the striking area to the extent where it prevents bruises and ill effects in later years. If you have ever observed certain Karate men practicing, look at their knuckles and you will sometimes notice the enlargement and disfiguring of the hand. This is due to the pounding and beating they take while using the makiwara board or other hard objects. After a long period of time the hands are left with little or no feeling at all. The medicine can help keep your hands normal in size without calloused knuckles or deforming of the hand.

In a very short period of time, with the proper training and instruction, one can obtain a great deal of proficiency in the Iron Palm art. But remember this is still not the ultimate of the art, there are other aspects which can cause unseen damages such as Dim Muk, or the Death Touch. The Iron Palm training can be taught on a physical level or in conjunction with the internal or Chi training. This depends on the instructor and how much he is willing to let out in the open.

Do not try any methods unless you have a competent instructor that can teach you the proper sequences. The worst thing you can do is to beat your hands to a pulp and not have any of the herbal medicine to relieve the ill effects from the striking.

Remember, imitating a person's feats doesn't necessarily mean you are doing it right. Understanding the principles is something that requires time and instruction.

> For one to be similar
> Is to be one in the same.
> But to be one different,
> One must understand how it is to be the same.

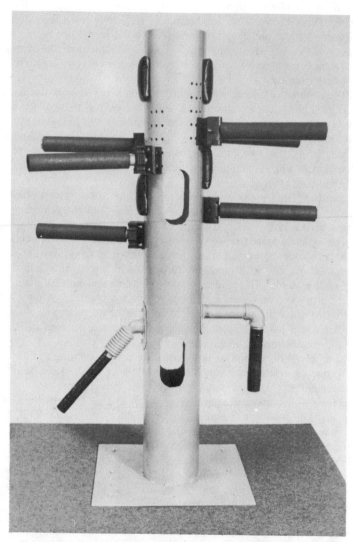

Using the equipment as a full size opponent. The two left sides are used for an opponent averaging in height about 5'5'' to 5'10'' — the opposite side for opponent averaging 5'10'' to 6'3''. The two kicking apparatus is used to develop power and accuracy.

The left side is a spring attachment which is used to develop a springy or snapping motion, while the right side is a solid pipe to develop sheer power.

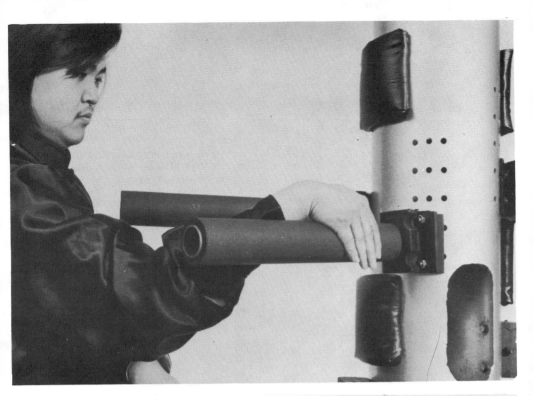

(Above) — Close up of hooking the equipment.

(Right) — Full shot of equipment with Sifu Wong working the equipment using a down-block and an outside wrist block on the top arm.

(Left) — **THE WOODEN BOARD DUMMY.** This equipment is used for practicing the various hand motions learned in Kung Fu. The three arms projecting outward represent different positioning of an opponent's punching hand.

(Below) — **SPINNING ARM.** Is used in developing speed necessary for fast reflexes and timing. The faster you hit the arm, the faster it spins around and striking back at different angles.

(Right) — AIR KICKING BAG. Showing proper way in holding the air bag. Position the leg into a square horse positioning with the top hand pushing forward and the bottom hand braces against the bottom half.

(Below) — The application of the equipment using a side heel thrust to develop power and distance.

HAMMER STRIKE — Ready position

Strike with the bottom portion of hand clenched in fist position.

INVERSE RIDGE HAND — Ready position

Twisting the hand in mid-air and strike with the inside edge of the hand.

IRON PALM — Ready position, hand flat.

Drop the hand straight down.

WILLOW PALM STRIKE — Ready position hand inverse palm up.

Strike downward on the side of the hand.

ELBOW STRIKE — Ready position

Strike downward with the upper forearm and elbow region.

FINGER STRIKE — Ready position

Strike down with the fingertips.

BACKHAND STRIKE — Hand up inhale.

Strike down and exhale using the back side of the hand.

TIGER CLAW — Ready position, claw hand above.

Strike down the fingertips.

Pressure Points

The body is one of nature's finest products. It is capable of building objects, creating music, or painting beautiful art work, but it is also sensitive to pain and illness.

It is strange how most fighters do not have any knowledge about the body's weak points or pressure points. These areas are used in the Chinese system to overcome an opponent with the minimum amount of force. The body is covered from head to toe with pressure points, some are more sensitive than others. The body is controlled by many different energy points which are in conjunction with the vital organs of the body. In China, the study of vital points and how to strike them is a special art by itself, which is known as Dim Muk or the "Death Touch". The art is still in existence today but is being taught only to the most trustworthy student that have proven themselves to their instructor. The art is not meant solely for disabling or killing a person, it is also involved in Chineses healing practices which covers acupunture and body massaging which is being practice the world over.

In Chinese Gung Fu systems there are 108 points used for disabling an opponent and 36 points use to kill an opponent. In acupunture there are 365 points used for healing and in older families system they have discover up to 1,000 points. The regulation of energy or chi is a direct relation of the breathing exercise which a good instructor will teach their students while others will just tell you not to worry about breathing. The understanding of the whole body is necessary to locate each vital point. The study of bone structure, vital organ, joints, muscles, and the nervous system is part of this section on Chinese medicine. You must learn how to relieve pain whenever it is necessary to help another individual and you must know how to do it quickly without injuring your patient.

Following is a chart on the various pressure point of the body and some application. Remember these various points because they will come in handy whenever you are in a fight but use them only if you need too. Remember there are other people out there that know more than you do, so don't go looking for trouble.

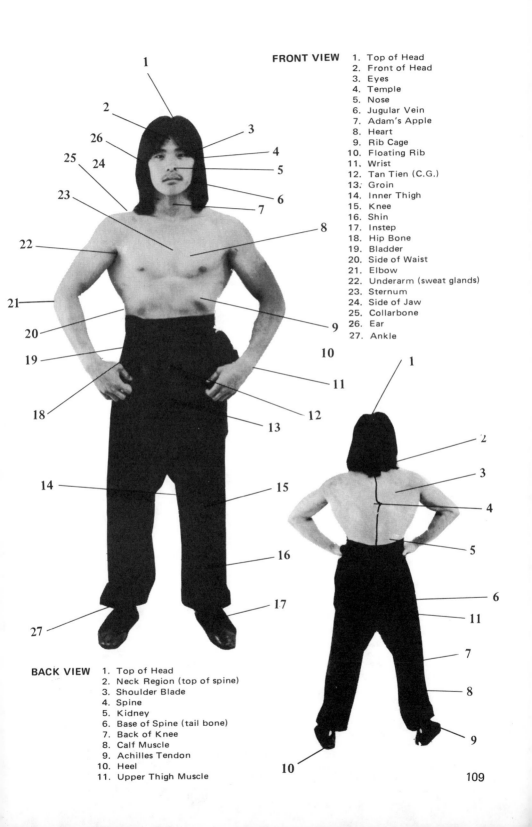

FRONT VIEW

1. Top of Head
2. Front of Head
3. Eyes
4. Temple
5. Nose
6. Jugular Vein
7. Adam's Apple
8. Heart
9. Rib Cage
10. Floating Rib
11. Wrist
12. Tan Tien (C.G.)
13. Groin
14. Inner Thigh
15. Knee
16. Shin
17. Instep
18. Hip Bone
19. Bladder
20. Side of Waist
21. Elbow
22. Underarm (sweat glands)
23. Sternum
24. Side of Jaw
25. Collarbone
26. Ear
27. Ankle

BACK VIEW

1. Top of Head
2. Neck Region (top of spine)
3. Shoulder Blade
4. Spine
5. Kidney
6. Base of Spine (tail bone)
7. Back of Knee
8. Calf Muscle
9. Achilles Tendon
10. Heel
11. Upper Thigh Muscle